Who Is
Wayne Gretzky?

Who Is
Wayne Gretzky?

By Gail Herman

Illustrated by Ted Hammond

Grosset & Dunlap

An Imprint of Penguin Group (USA) LLC

For Bennett, Wayne Gretzky of the Wii—GH

To Dad and Wendy—TH

GROSSET & DUNLAP
Published by the Penguin Group
Penguin Group (USA) LLC, 375 Hudson Street, New York, New York 10014, USA

USA | Canada | UK | Ireland | Australia | New Zealand | India | South Africa | China

penguin.com
A Penguin Random House Company

Text copyright © 2015 by Gail Herman. Illustrations copyright © 2015 by Ted Hammond. Cover illustration copyright © 2015 by Nancy Harrison. All rights reserved. Published by Grosset & Dunlap, a division of Penguin Young Readers Group, 345 Hudson Street, New York, New York 10014. GROSSET & DUNLAP is a trademark of Penguin Group (USA) LLC. Printed in the USA.

Library of Congress Cataloging-in-Publication Data is available.

ISBN 978-0-448-48321-4   10 9 8 7 6 5 4 3 2 1

Contents

Who Is Wayne Gretzky?....................................1

Growing Up Gretzky..9

Playing Up...23

Leaving Home...32

Number Ninety-Nine.......................................39

In the Big Leagues...46

Here We Go, Oilers!..56

Wayne, Meet Stanley.......................................64

Dynasties and Dating.......................................70

Beginnings and Endings...................................77

Now a King..82

Last Years on Ice..88

Still the Greatest...97

Timelines..102

Bibliography...104

Top Records..106

Who Is
Wayne Gretzky?

Fifty in fifty. That means scoring fifty goals in fifty hockey games. Maurice "The Rocket" Richard, of the Montreal Canadiens, was the first National Hockey League player to do it, in the 1944–1945 season.

Ten years passed. Twenty. Thirty. It seemed no other hockey player could pull off the feat. Finally New York Islander Mike Bossy tied the record thirty-six years later.

How much time would pass before someone else scored fifty goals in fifty games?

One season later, Wayne Gretzky, just twenty years old, skated onto the ice. The place: Northlands Coliseum in Edmonton, Canada. The date: December 30, 1981.

Wayne was the center for the Edmonton Oilers. He was about to face off against the Philadelphia Flyers.

It had been an amazing season for Wayne. By the thirteenth game, he had thirteen goals. After thirty-five games, he had thirty-eight goals. And after thirty-eight games? He had a whopping forty-five.

Now he was ready for game thirty-nine.

No one—ever—had scored fifty goals in less than fifty games. Just five more goals and Wayne would do it.

On this gusty winter day, Wayne felt lucky. Somehow he knew he'd score—and score big.

In the first period he scored two goals, one right after the other. By the end of the second period, he scored again for a hat trick: three goals altogether. Five minutes into the third period, Wayne slid the puck around a rushing defender. He shot, lifting the puck high in the air. He scored! His fourth goal of the game!

Now Wayne had forty-nine goals. Could he make it fifty?

With ten minutes left, Wayne shot and shot again. Each one was stopped by the Flyers' goalie. Only seconds remained. The game was close: Oilers, 6; Flyers, 5.

Philadelphia pulled its goalie off the ice. An offensive player skated out, to try to tie the game. It was a risk. Philadelphia left their net wide open. Wayne took off down the ice.

Grant Fuhr, the Oilers' goalie, pushed the puck to right wing Glenn Anderson.

"Pass it to me!" Wayne shouted from the Flyers' zone. Three seconds were left on the clock. Wayne got the puck. A defender charged. Two seconds left. Wayne zipped around the Flyer. He shot.

Goal!

Wayne had done it. Fifty goals in only thirty-nine games.

Teammates mobbed Wayne. The hometown
crowd went crazy. Wayne Gretzky didn't just
break the record. He destroyed it! By game fifty,
he had sixty-one goals. And by the end of the
season, Wayne scored ninety-two goals in eighty
games for another record.

Wayne would go on to break or tie more than sixty records. Most goals in a season and most goals in a career. Most assists in a season and most assists in a career. Most career points. (In hockey, players earn a point for each goal or assist.) If you only counted Wayne's assists, he'd still have the most points of any player. Ever.

Wayne retired in 1999. He hasn't played for years. Yet many of his records still stand—including fifty goals in thirty-nine games. He probably holds the record for holding the most records of any professional athlete.

Wayne wasn't the biggest or fastest or strongest. But the way he played—his style and smarts—would change the game. Wayne Douglas Gretzky was a different kind of hockey player, almost from the time he could walk.

Chapter 1
Growing Up Gretzky

In Canada, hockey is THE sport. When Canadian children dream of being a pro athlete, most don't think of baseball or football. They dream of hockey, and playing for glory in the National Hockey League. It's said Canadian children grow up on skates. Wayne Gretzky did. He started skating when he learned to walk.

Wayne was born on January 26, 1961, in Brantford, a small city in the province of Ontario, Canada. In Brantford, it snows for almost half the year. There's lots of time to skate outdoors.

When Wayne was two, his dad bought him his first pair of skates. Walter Gretzky strapped them on for little Wayne. Together, they stepped onto the frozen Nith River.

Walter helped Wayne slide along the ice. According to Walter, "He'd never ever been on skates before. I put him on the ice. He literally skated. Just skated." And that's where it all began—on the river running right past the Gretzky family farm.

Walter Gretzky had grown up on the farm, outside town. He too grew up playing hockey. He met Wayne's mom, Phyllis, when he was a teenager. Phyllis went to the games he played. And Walter watched Phyllis play softball. Sports were always a part of their lives.

The two married in 1960, and moved to a small house in Brantford.

PROVINCES AND TERRITORIES

IN LAND AREA, CANADA IS THE SECOND-BIGGEST COUNTRY IN THE WORLD. (RUSSIA IS THE BIGGEST; THE UNITED STATES IS THE THIRD.) BUT WHILE THE UNITED STATES IS DIVIDED INTO FIFTY STATES, CANADA IS MADE UP OF TEN PROVINCES AND THREE TERRITORIES. THE PROVINCES—INCLUDING ONTARIO, QUEBEC, AND BRITISH COLUMBIA—

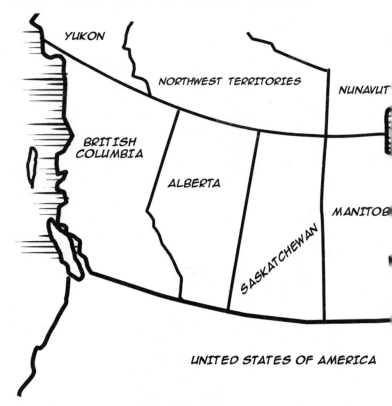

ARE SIMILAR TO STATES. PROVINCES MAKE UP
60 PERCENT OF CANADA'S LAND, AND 97 PERCENT
OF ITS POPULATION. FEW PEOPLE LIVE IN THE
TERRITORIES TO THE NORTH. WHY? LIKE IN THE
LARGEST US STATE, ALASKA, THE ARCTIC WEATHER
THERE IS HARSH. THE NUNAVUT TERRITORY
STRETCHES TO THE NORTH POLE!

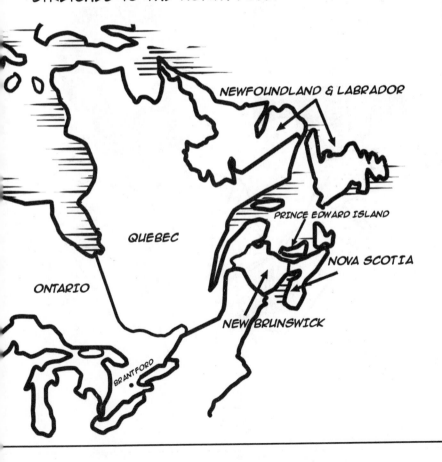

NEWFOUNDLAND & LABRADOR

PRINCE EDWARD ISLAND

QUEBEC

NOVA SCOTIA

ONTARIO

NEW BRUNSWICK

BRANTFORD

The city is known as the birthplace of the telephone. It's where Alexander Graham Bell worked on his landmark invention. The first telephone factory was built there, too. Phones were big business. And many people worked for Bell Canada. Walter was a lineman for the company.

ALEXANDER
GRAHAM BELL

In 1961,
Walter was
working above
a manhole. A
phone cable
had caught,
and Walter
was trying
to loosen it.
He pulled.
Suddenly, a
heavy frame flew

out of the manhole. It hit Walter on the head,
cracking his helmet. The next thing he knew, he
was lying facedown on the street. Everything was
spinning. He had a fractured skull.

The accident left Walter deaf in one ear. He
had constant headaches. But Walter Gretzky
didn't let that stop him. How could he? He and
Phyllis had a growing family.

After Wayne, Walter and Phyllis had four more children: Kim, Keith, Brent, and Glen. On weekends, they'd all troop out to the family farm to visit their grandparents.

Every Sunday after church, Grandma Gretzky made a huge dinner. She was born in Poland. So she served traditional Polish food like pierogi, a kind of dumpling. And every Saturday night, from the time Wayne was little, the family gathered around the TV. They watched a show called *Hockey Night in Canada*.

While the TV was on, Wayne and Grandma had their own face-off. Grandma, the goalie, sat in a chair. Toddler Wayne "skated" across the floor, shoeless. Using a tiny hockey stick, he'd shoot a rubber ball or rolled-up sock between Grandma's legs.

Wayne was hooked on hockey.

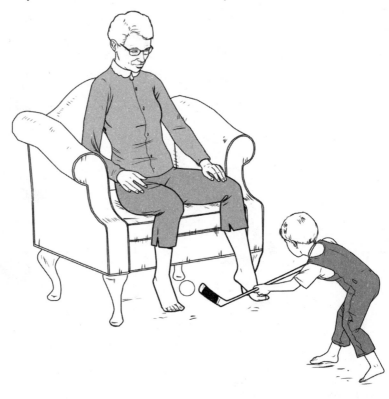

In town, Walter took Wayne to park rinks. Wayne never wanted to leave. Poor Walter waited for hours in the freezing cold. When Wayne was four, Walter had an idea. He'd turn their backyard into a skating rink.

First he cut the grass very short. Then he turned on the sprinkler. He let it run all night long. In the morning, the ground was covered in a layer of ice. It was a rink! Now Walter could sit in his warm kitchen and watch Wayne out the window. The family called it "Wally Coliseum."

HISTORY OF HOCKEY

IT'S CALLED "THE FASTEST GAME ON EARTH."
BUT HOCKEY DEVELOPED SLOWLY OVER TIME.
BASED ON ANCIENT BALL-AND-STICK GAMES FROM
AROUND THE WORLD, IT GREW INTO THE MODERN
SPORT IN CANADA. IN MONTREAL IN 1875, JAMES
CREIGHTON PUT TOGETHER THE FIRST ORGANIZED
INDOOR GAME WITH RULES, INCLUDING USING A
WOODEN PUCK INSTEAD OF A BALL.

JAMES CREIGHTON

Wayne wanted to learn everything about playing hockey. So Walter set up empty detergent bottles. He taught Wayne to weave around them. He ran through drills. "Go where the puck is going," he told Wayne again and again. "Not where it's been." Sometimes Wayne used a tennis ball instead of a puck. It taught him control.

But Wayne wanted to play in real games. He begged his father to find him a team.

Wayne was too young, his parents thought. He was only five. Back then, players had to be at least ten. But Wayne kept begging. So his parents tried to sign him up for the Brantford Atom league team. They were turned away.

Wayne didn't give up. He kept practicing. And he kept after his parents.

The next year Wayne turned six. This time, he was allowed to try out. Wayne was small— even for his age. But all those drills paid off. His skills made him stand out. And he made the team!

Chapter 2
Playing Up

In Wayne's league, the uniforms were made for older, bigger kids. The top hung past his knees. It caught on his hockey stick. It made it hard to shoot. So Walter tucked the right side of the uniform— Wayne's shooting side— into his pants. It became Wayne's special look, right up to his final NHL game.

That first year, six-year-old Wayne scored just one goal. Everyone on his team won a trophy. Except for Wayne. After the awards ceremony, he cried.

Walter told Wayne to keep practicing. Keep working hard. And soon he'd have more trophies than he could imagine.

Wayne listened. He practiced longer and harder. The next year he scored twenty-seven goals. The following year, 104.

How did he improve? Every winter, whenever he could, Wayne would be outside skating. As he grew older, he'd skate before school and after school. He'd eat dinner in skates.

Then he'd go out again in the dark, a floodlight shining on the yard. Finally, at around 10:00 p.m., his mom and dad would insist Wayne come inside.

In the warm weather, Wayne didn't stop. He hit pucks against the family farmhouse. Of course, Wayne broke a few windows. Once, his grandfather had just put in a new glass pane. Wayne let a puck fly. *Crash!* Broken again.

Wayne practiced for hours on his own. But on weekends, neighborhood kids came to the backyard rink. He played against them all—

no matter how old or how tough. And when they wanted to take a break and go to the movies? Wayne stayed on the ice.

No one told him to practice. Not his father, not his mother. He just loved it.

When Wayne turned ten, the same age as the other players in the league, he scored 378 goals! It was a youth scoring record! The entire country took notice.

Canadian newspaper reporters called Wayne "The Great One" and "The Great Gretzky." The nicknames stuck. Wayne didn't really like them. He liked "Gretz." That's what his friends called him.

Wayne felt embarrassed by the fuss. Confident on the ice, he was quiet off. He didn't talk a lot. He didn't like the spotlight.

Still, there were interviews on radio and TV. Dinners and award shows. Banners hung at away games. They said, "See Wayne Gretzky, ten-year-old scoring ace." Kids his own age asked for his autograph.

Sometimes, going into games, Wayne switched team jackets with another player so people wouldn't stop him. At home, no one paid any more attention to him than to his brothers or sister. And that's how he liked it.

Wayne's family didn't have a lot of money. Their home was small. Wayne shared a room with his brothers. It was barely big enough for the beds.

But Wayne's parents did whatever they could for their children. And they put a lot into hockey.

SPORTS AND THE GRETZKY SIBLINGS

KEITH, FIVE YEARS YOUNGER THAN WAYNE, PLAYED AND COACHED FOR MINOR LEAGUE HOCKEY TEAMS. HE WAS NAMED DIRECTOR OF AMATEUR SCOUTING FOR THE BOSTON BRUINS IN 2013. BRENT, TWELVE YEARS YOUNGER THAN WAYNE, PLAYED FOR THE NHL'S TAMPA BAY LIGHTNING FROM 1993 TO 1995. HE FACED OFF AGAINST WAYNE IN HIS SECOND GAME AS A PRO. GLEN WAS BORN SEVEN YEARS AFTER WAYNE, WITH A TWISTED FOOT THAT COULDN'T BE PUT FLAT ON THE GROUND. HE WASN'T ABLE TO PLAY MUCH ORGANIZED HOCKEY. BUT ACCORDING TO WAYNE, GLEN PRACTICED EVEN HARDER THAN HE DID. KIM, ONLY TWO YEARS YOUNGER, EXCELLED AT TRACK-AND-FIELD SPORTS GROWING UP.

KIM, KEITH, GLEN, AND BRENT GRETZKY

They gave up eating in restaurants and buying new curtains to pay for hockey equipment and fees—not only for Wayne but for his brothers, too.

"You're not better than anyone else," his parents kept reminding Wayne. "Everyone is equal. Some are just more fortunate than others."

Wayne was always a regular kid. He had friends. He fished. He swam. He played lacrosse and baseball during hockey's off-season.

He dreamed of pitching for his favorite team, the Detroit Tigers. He didn't stop playing baseball until he turned pro in hockey. The Toronto Blue Jays even offered Wayne a tryout when he was a teenager. But in Brantford, all eyes were on Wayne in the hockey rink.

Chapter 3
Leaving Home

Walter coached Wayne and his teammates for years. But when Wayne turned ten, Walter stopped. He thought other parents would complain. They'd think it wasn't fair that Wayne got so much playing time.

Even with a new coach, Wayne got lots of ice time. Some parents did resent it. What about *their* kids? They didn't like Wayne's growing fame, either.

They called him a puck hog and other names. They booed when he skated onto the ice. He wasn't even that good, they claimed. All those goals and assists? Just luck.

Wayne felt pressure from so many adults putting him down. He thought they were wrong.

He played fair. He passed the puck when it was
the right move. He wasn't selfish. And he had a
high assist record to prove it.

Wayne grew even quieter, afraid to say anything to make the situation worse. But he realized he had a responsibility. People came to watch him play. He had to try his best in every game. And as hard as it was to answer questions, he had to talk to interviewers. It was all part of playing hockey.

Wayne still watched *Hockey Night* on TV. Now, though, he was serious about strategy—how to win a game. He drew a rink on a pad, and followed moves with his pencil. He studied plays.

He wanted to know why the puck went one way and not the other. He understood it was all about angles.

Wayne's game improved a lot. But hockey wasn't fun anymore. It was hard to play in Brantford. Everyone had an opinion about him.

When he was fourteen, Wayne was invited to join a junior team in Toronto, the largest city in Canada. Toronto was an hour away. Wayne would have to play lots of late games. He'd have to move away from home.

His parents didn't like the idea. Again, they thought Wayne was too young. Wayne, however, convinced them he was ready.

Living with family friends would be fine, he insisted. Finally Walter and Phyllis agreed.

Wayne signed with a Junior B team, a high-level amateur team, just below semipro. He'd go on to win Rookie of the Year.

Even better, Wayne was making friends at his new school in Toronto. He wasn't the Great Gretzky. There, he was just Gretz. Some kids didn't even know he played hockey!

Still, it was difficult being away from home. For two months, Wayne cried himself to sleep. He couldn't wait to go home every weekend. His youngest brother, Brent, was only three years old. Wayne didn't want Brent to grow up not knowing him.

In 1977, Wayne turned sixteen. Now he could play Junior A hockey. Junior A is semipro, one step away from the pros. But he'd have to move again. Everyone hoped it would be close to home.

That didn't happen. Wayne wound up in Sault Ste. Marie, 480 miles away.

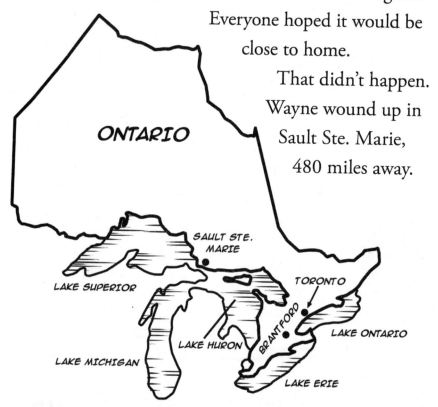

Chapter 4
Number Ninety-Nine

Junior A hockey is rough. Players want to make the pros. They skate fast and check hard. Young and small, Wayne knew this was a true test. Would players laugh at his size? Well, so what if they did? They might as well laugh at his uniform number, too, he figured.

Wayne had always wanted to wear number nine. That was hockey great Gordie Howe's number, and Gordie was Wayne's idol. But here— at "the Soo," as Sault Ste. Marie was called—nine was already taken.

GORDIE HOWE

Wayne's coach suggested he wear "double nines." Ninety-nine. It was unusual then. Players' numbers didn't often go above thirty-one. But if anyone laughed at Wayne's number, they stopped when they saw him play.

Wayne had a crazy schedule. The team flew to away games in small run-down planes. Once in the fog, their plane brushed the treetops. No wonder Wayne wound up with a fear of flying!

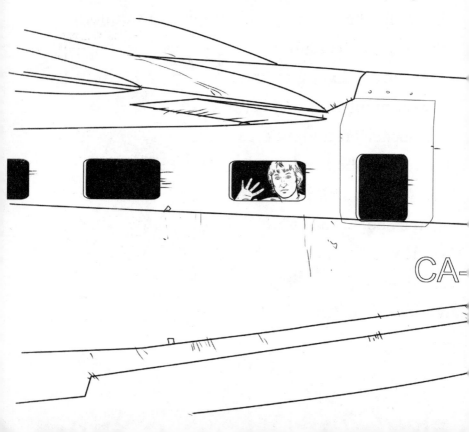

Wayne was staying with another family. And sometimes, he wouldn't arrive home until 3:00 a.m. He slept for a few hours. Then he went to class at the local high school. For all that, he was paid only twenty-five dollars a week. Wayne didn't care about the money. For him, it was all about the game. Yes, he studied at school. "Great in math, terrible in English," he revealed in his autobiography.

And he went for pie and ice cream every day after school. But other than that, he practiced, practiced, practiced. He never had a girlfriend. He didn't go to the prom.

Was it worth it?

At the end of the season, he was the top junior player in Canada. He won the Rookie of the Year and Most Sportsmanlike awards. He broke the single-season scoring record. He was featured in *Sports Illustrated* and the *New York Times*.

Fans marveled at his skill. He seemed to know where the puck was going. He could pass without even looking. It was like he had hockey ESP.

Wayne knew better. Sure, he had natural talent. But mostly it was all those drills in his backyard. Plain hard work.

Again, some people wrote off Wayne's season as luck. He was so scrawny! So small! He couldn't even skate that fast. He'd never make it on a professional team, critics said.

All that made Wayne even more determined. He wanted to go pro. The NHL wouldn't consider him. They had rules; players had to be twenty years old. Wayne was only seventeen.

But in 1978 there was another league: the World Hockey Association. Started in 1971, the league had older pros like Gordie Howe and fresh new players.

Wayne signed with the Indianapolis Racers, which was part of the WHA. He'd be living in the United States now. He was set to earn more than three quarters of a million dollars. And he was still in high school! Over the years, Wayne would try to buy his parents cars and homes, expensive things they couldn't afford. But they never let him. They wouldn't move out of Wayne's childhood home. They still drove their old station wagon. And his dad kept working for the phone company.

Wayne thought he'd settle in Indiana for a good long time. But he only played eight games.

And then he was traded to another team in the WHA. Once again, he got on a plane. He only had the clothes on his back, his hockey gear, an extra pair of pants, and a toothbrush. He wasn't even sure where he was going. But once in the air, he found out.

Wayne Gretzky was on his way to the Edmonton Oilers and hockey glory.

Chapter 5
In the Big Leagues

Edmonton is the capital of the Canadian province Alberta. Edmonton is farther north than any other city with a pro hockey team.

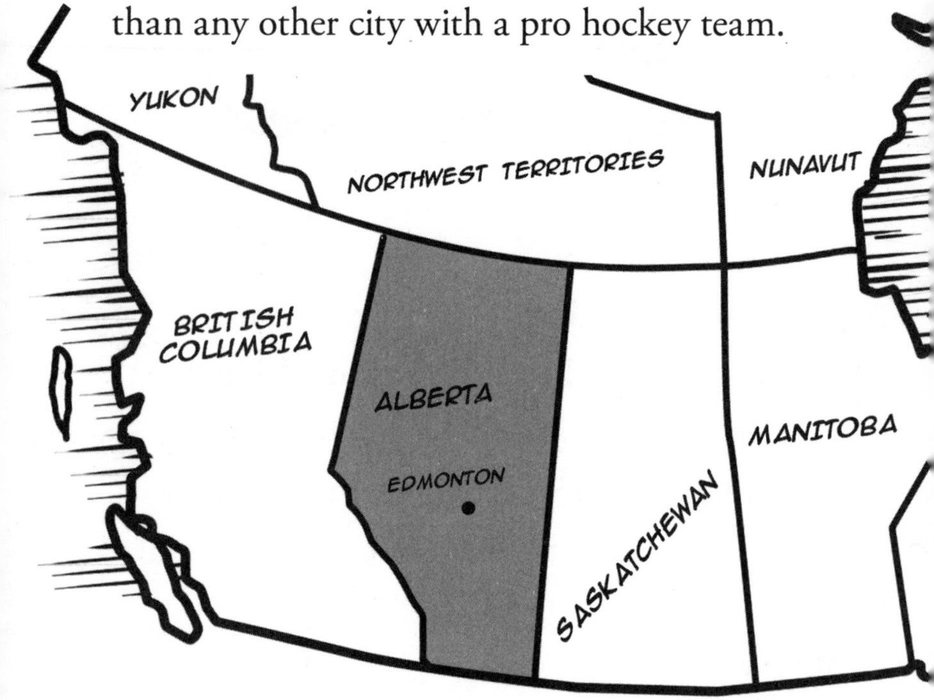

YUKON

NORTHWEST TERRITORIES

NUNAVUT

BRITISH COLUMBIA

ALBERTA

EDMONTON

MANITOBA

SASKATCHEWAN

And in 1979, it seemed worlds away from the center of the sport. But the city of Edmonton was growing. Its oil industry, begun in 1947, was hotter than ever. And the people loved hockey. They couldn't wait for the WHA season to begin in October.

GLEN SATHER

Glen Sather, the Oilers' coach, took a quick look at seventeen-year-old Wayne. Skinny. Long hair. Young.

In fact, the whole team was new and young. And they didn't take themselves too seriously. For Wayne's eighteenth birthday, a huge cake was brought onto center ice. Later, back in the locker room, one of the guys sat on it!

Unfortunately, the next year the WHA went out of business. Some teams folded. Not the Oilers. They took a step up and joined the NHL. At eighteen, Wayne became part of the NHL.

When Wayne joined the NHL, he found the players stronger and tougher than any he'd yet faced. They were the best in the world. Once again, critics pointed a finger at Wayne. Yes, he had done fine in the WHA. But he wouldn't cut it in the NHL.

Wayne didn't let the comments get to him. As always, he tried even harder. Luckily, the young Oilers had grown. They had defenseman Kevin Lowe and center Mark Messier. Wayne became great friends with both.

THE NATIONAL HOCKEY LEAGUE

THE NHL FORMED IN 1917 WITH ONLY FIVE TEAMS, ALL FROM CANADA: THE MONTREAL CANADIENS, THE MONTREAL WANDERERS, THE OTTAWA SENATORS, THE QUEBEC BULLDOGS, AND THE TORONTO ARENAS, RENAMED THE MAPLE LEAFS IN 1927. OVER TIME, THE LEAGUE GREW TO INCLUDE US TEAMS, WITH THE BOSTON BRUINS THE FIRST TO JOIN IN 1924. THE NHL SHRANK DURING WORLD WAR II, THEN GREW AGAIN. TODAY, IT'S THE TOP HOCKEY LEAGUE IN THE WORLD, WITH THIRTY TEAMS, TWENTY-THREE IN THE UNITED STATES AND SEVEN IN CANADA. THE TEAMS ARE DIVIDED INTO TWO CONFERENCES, THE EASTERN (WITH THE METROPOLITAN AND ATLANTIC DIVISIONS) AND WESTERN (WITH THE PACIFIC AND CENTRAL DIVISIONS).

VANCOUVER CANUCKS

SAN JOSE SHARKS

LOS ANGELES KINGS

ANAHEIM DUCKS

It wasn't an easy year. Wayne had a bad sore throat for most of the season. He lost weight. He lived on aspirin and cough drops. Still, Wayne finished the season tied for scoring leader with the Los Angeles Kings' Marcel Dionne. And he started his collection of NHL awards: the Hart Trophy for Most Valuable Player and the Lady Byng Trophy for most gentlemanly player. The Lady Byng meant a lot to Wayne.

MARK MESSIER

MARK "THE MOOSE" MESSIER GREW UP IN EDMONTON, PART OF A HOCKEY-PLAYING FAMILY. AT SIXTEEN, WEIGHING TWO HUNDRED POUNDS, HE STARTED PLAYING FOR A JUNIOR LEAGUE TEAM. CLEARLY TALENTED, MESSIER WENT STRAIGHT TO THE PROS, THE WHA'S RACERS, THEN THE CINCINNATI STINGERS. LATER, HE SIGNED WITH THE OILERS, THE NEW YORK RANGERS, AND THEN THE VANCOUVER CANUCKS. HE WAS BACK WITH THE RANGERS BEFORE RETIRING IN 2004. RECENTLY, HE'S WORKED ON A PROJECT TO BUILD A HOCKEY CENTER IN THE BRONX TO HELP YOUNG NEW YORK CITY PLAYERS AND THEIR COMMUNITY. MESSIER WILL ALWAYS BE KNOWN FOR HIS OFFENSIVE *AND* DEFENSIVE SKILLS; HE IS THE ONLY CAPTAIN TO LEAD TWO DIFFERENT TEAMS—THE OILERS AND RANGERS—TO CHAMPIONSHIPS.

Right from the start, Wayne spoke out against players fighting in hockey. He knew fans expected to see big tough guys going at each other.

But he didn't think it had to be part of the game. In fact, he stayed away from fights—then and throughout his career.

Chapter 6
Here We Go, Oilers!

The Oilers were a team to watch. In the next season's playoffs, they beat the Montreal Canadiens, winner of twenty-two championship titles at that time.

In baseball's World Series, the winning team gets their own Commissioner's Trophy. In the NHL, every team shares one trophy: the Stanley Cup. Each year, it's passed on to the new winners.

In the first game of the season's playoffs, Wayne got five assists. A playoff record! He led his team to sweep the series. It's still one of the biggest upsets in hockey history.

The Oilers went on to face the defending champions, the New York Islanders.

Wayne and his teammates were excited. The entire team sat on the bench and chanted like fans, "Here we go, Oilers. Here we go."

They lost. The Stanley Cup went to the
Islanders. But the Oilers had proved themselves.

Each season, teams play about eighty games.
In 1981–1982, Wayne dominated almost every one
he was in. He broke record after record. Goals.
Assists. Scoring streaks.

THE STANLEY CUP

THE NHL TROPHY IS NAMED FOR FREDERICK ARTHUR STANLEY, AN ENGLISH LORD. LORD STANLEY CAME TO CANADA AS GOVERNOR GENERAL AND QUICKLY BECAME A HOCKEY FAN. IN 1892, HE BOUGHT A PUNCH BOWL FOR FIFTY DOLLARS, AND GAVE IT TO THE TOP AMATEUR HOCKEY TEAM. LATER IT WAS AWARDED TO PRO TEAMS, FINALLY SERVING AS THE NHL PRIZE. ALL WINNING PLAYERS, COACHES, OWNERS, AND STAFF MEMBERS ARE LISTED ON THE CUP, WHICH WAS REMADE IN 1958. WHEN THE TROPHY RUNS OUT OF SPACE, THE OLDEST TEAM IS TAKEN OFF. MISTAKES HAVE BEEN MADE: CANADIENS GOALIE JACQUES PLANTE WON THE CUP FIVE TIMES, AND EACH TIME HIS NAME WAS SPELLED DIFFERENTLY. EVERY TEAM MEMBER GETS TO KEEP THE CUP FOR A DAY. IT'S BEEN TO RESTAURANTS, HOMES, STADIUMS, EVEN IN A SWIMMING POOL WITH HOCKEY GREAT MARIO LEMIEUX. THE STANLEY CUP IS UNLIKE ANY OTHER PRO-LEAGUE TROPHY.

The area behind the net was nicknamed "Gretzky's office." No other player used the space like Wayne. He would wait there patiently, holding the puck. When he saw the right pass? *Bang*—he slid the puck to a teammate for a goal.

Or he banked it off the goalie, or the net, or the boards, to score. Magazines called him the best player in the NHL. He starred in commercials for soda and sportswear. Over the years, his fame grew. He had his own cereal and

his own doll. He appeared on talk shows, a soap opera, and other TV programs. By 1991, there was even a cartoon series with "Wayne Gretzky."

But after three seasons in the NHL, his team had yet to win the Stanley Cup.

Chapter 7
Wayne, Meet Stanley

Wayne became captain of the Oilers before the 1983–1984 season. Still quiet, he tried to lead by example. He paid attention to everyone, from the oldest player to the youngest; to each and every locker room attendant.

Wayne had been playing in major professional leagues for five years. For luck, he liked to do things the same way before each game.

He always got dressed in the same order. Left shin pad, left outer pad. Then the right. And so on. Finally, he tucked in the right side of his jersey. He even tried to eat the same foods for his pregame meal.

Superstitious? Maybe. But in 1984, Wayne could really see the Oilers winning the

championship. He could feel it. "Nothing I've ever done means more than this," he told his teammates. The Oilers made it to the finals, a best-of-seven series. Their opponents: the Islanders, again.

This was Wayne's chance. But the Islanders shadowed him every second. Wayne didn't score in the first three games. It was a playoff slump. Still, the Oilers were up two games to one.

In the fourth game, Wayne used an old trick: He waited half a second to pass the puck. The Islanders' defense was thrown. When the puck came back to Wayne, he "deked"—faked out—

the other player again. Then he shot the puck
backhand, right into the net.

The pressure off, Wayne played with a new
fury. He fought through check after check until
he scored again. It was a huge victory for the
Oilers. But they needed to win the next game for
the Cup.

It was May 19, 1984. A home game. Twice,

teammate Jari Kurri passed the puck to Wayne. And twice Wayne drove the puck into the net. He assisted on a third goal. By the end of the second period, the Oilers were up 4–0. But then in the third period—*bang, bang*—the Islanders scored twice. The score: 4–2. Now the Islanders had the momentum.

Emotions ran high. The pressure was on. But the Oilers held strong. They scored again. The crowd roared. With seconds left on the clock, they counted down the time: "Five, four, three, two, one!"

Game over! The Oilers had won the
championship! Streamers and balloons fell from
the ceiling. Wayne and his Oilers teammates
raced toward one another for a giant group hug.
Fans swarmed the ice. Wayne's little brother Brent
jumped into his arms.

On TV, millions watched Captain Gretzky lift the Stanley Cup, then skate around the rink.

Afterward, Wayne and his teammates took "Stanley" for a walk. They went all around Edmonton, to restaurants, parks, and hospitals. Wayne wanted to share the prize with the people of the city. Everyone was part of the victory, he felt. His teammates. His family. The fans. Because he couldn't have done it alone.

Chapter 8
Dynasties and Dating

Wayne and the Oilers won the Stanley Cup again the next year, 1985. They seemed a shoo-in for 1986, too. That division series against the Calgary Flames went to seven games.

Five minutes into the third period of the seventh game, the score was tied. Oilers defenseman Steve Smith skated to the net to stop a goal by the Flames. He tried to clear the puck.

But the puck hit the Oilers' goalie, Grant Fuhr, on the leg. Then it bounced into the net. The Flames didn't even have to shoot. It was an own goal for the Oilers. Calgary won.

Steve Smith sat on the bench and cried.

But Wayne knew the loss wasn't Steve's fault. They played as a team. And they lost as a team. Next season they'd come back stronger. And he was right.

The Oilers won the cup in 1987. Right away,
Wayne handed the trophy to Steve Smith. He
wanted Steve to be among the first to raise it high.

In 1988, the Oilers won yet again. Four championships in five years. People called the team a dynasty. Wayne Gretzky—with his trophies, records, and leadership—was the most famous person in Canada.

In spring 1987, Wayne went to a Los Angeles Lakers basketball game. American actress and dancer Janet Jones came over to say hello. The two had met over the years.

But now Janet and Wayne really talked. They realized they had a lot in common. Both came from large families. Both had careers at a very young age. They knew the good and bad that came from being famous. And they knew they wanted a normal life, with lots of kids. They fell in love.

Janet had never seen a hockey game. Right away she loved the excitement of the sport. She cheered Wayne on all through the 1987–1988 season, and his fourth title with the Oilers.

JANET JONES

JANET JONES GREW UP OUTSIDE OF ST. LOUIS, MISSOURI, THE SECOND YOUNGEST OF SEVEN CHILDREN. A TOMBOY, JANET PLAYED SOFTBALL AS A YOUNG GIRL. BUT HER REAL LOVE WAS DANCE. SHE MOVED TO HOLLYWOOD, FINDING WORK AS A MODEL AND DANCING ON THE TV SHOW *DANCE FEVER*. MOVIES FOLLOWED; HER MOST FAMOUS ROLES WERE IN *THE FLAMINGO KID* IN 1984, THE GYMNASTICS MOVIE *AMERICAN ANTHEM* IN 1986, AND AS A PITCHER IN THE BASEBALL MOVIE *A LEAGUE OF THEIR OWN* IN 1992.

But things were shaky with the team. The owner was having money troubles. Wayne was paid $1 million a year. Soon his salary would go up to at least $5 million. The Oilers could save a lot of money if he wasn't on the team. And they could get millions by trading him. There were rumblings of a change.

Wayne's family tried to keep the rumors from Wayne. And Wayne blocked out any news. He wanted to focus on hockey. Not business.

And when the championship season ended, Wayne had something else to think about. He and Janet were getting married!

Chapter 9
Beginnings and Endings

The wedding was held in Edmonton, on July 16, 1988. It was such big news, the ceremony was broadcast live on TV. Newspapers called it Canada's Royal Wedding.

Ten thousand fans lined the streets outside the cathedral. Seven hundred guests sat inside. Hundreds of reporters crammed the aisles. Wayne later said he felt more nervous during the ceremony than in any game seven of the playoffs.

Soon after, Wayne and Janet left on a trip to California. They stayed at the home of Canadian actor and friend Alan Thicke. The newlyweds babysat Alan's son Robin, who would go on to become a famous pop singer.

By now Wayne knew he was going to be traded. He thought the Los Angeles Kings would be the best fit.

The news broke on August 9, 1988: Wayne Gretzky was no longer an Edmonton Oiler. He was an LA King.

Canadian TV programs were interrupted. The announcement was headline news across Canada. People called it the "Trade of the Century" or just "the Trade." Say those words today? Canadians would likely still know you were talking about Wayne Gretzky.

The news shocked Canadians. Wayne was a national symbol . . . and he was going to the United States!

Some blamed Janet. They said she forced the move. She wanted to be close to Hollywood and the movie business. Most, though, blamed the Oilers' owner. Outraged, they protested in the streets. But the deal was done.

For Wayne, it was a very tough time. He'd miss his teammates. They'd almost grown up together. Would he ever be that close with the LA players? With the staff?

There was one Oilers staff member that Wayne worried about most of all. Years earlier, he had found a job for a young man named Joey Moss. Joey had Down syndrome. Before leaving the team, Wayne made sure Joey would always have a job in the locker room.

The Oilers' owner called a press conference.
At the podium, Wayne answered questions from
reporters. He spoke about his family. How he and
Janet were expecting their first child. But he broke
down in tears, and had to stop. He never finished
the press conference.

Chapter 10
Now a King

In Los Angeles, the mood was very different. People were excited about the trade—even people who never paid attention to hockey. Wayne posed

with LA Lakers basketball star Magic Johnson for the cover of *Sports Illustrated*. Ticket sales for the Kings tripled. The hockey arena, usually half empty, would be filled with fans.

But the Kings were fourth in their division. The team had begun playing in 1967 and had never won their division. Could one player change all that?

Yes! With one goal and three assists in the very

first game, Wayne led his new team to victory.
Now movie stars, athletes, and everyone else in
the city was a Kings fan. Hollywood became
"Hockeywood." Hockey fever spread from LA
to other US towns and cities. More games were
televised. More hockey teams sprang up. And kids
were signing up to play like never before.

Wayne became the face of hockey. He was always polite, always friendly. He looked like a regular guy, not a big bruiser with muscles to match.

That season, the Kings rose to second place. And Wayne grew to feel comfortable with his new team and his new city. It was all so different from Edmonton. Here in California, there'd be no snowy winters. Wayne could drive to practice with the top down on his convertible.

In LA, there were so many famous people, Wayne didn't stand out. He liked the privacy. And he loved his growing family. Daughter Paulina was born in 1988.

As for hockey, Wayne was adding to the record books. But in the autumn of 1991, Wayne felt unhappy. It was the start of the season. And already he felt beat up. Even worse, he wasn't scoring—at all!

In October, Wayne talked to his dad on the phone, just like he did almost every day. Walter could always cheer up Wayne. And the phone call helped.

But soon after, Wayne got another call.

It was his sister, Kim. Their dad had collapsed. He was in the hospital with a brain aneurysm, a tear in a blood vessel. It might be fatal.

Immediately, Wayne hired a private plane. He flew his family to the Ontario hospital. Walter wasn't expected to make it through the night.

Fortunately, surgery saved his life. Wayne missed game after game, staying with his dad. It would take time for Walter to get better, he learned. And his memory would never be the same.

The stress on Wayne didn't help his game. He was still in a slump. And he hated playing badly. He thought about quitting. He couldn't talk to his dad about it. So he spoke to Janet, Mark Messier, and his coaches. And Wayne turned it around.

One game in Toronto, he scored a goal and had three assists. After, he visited his dad.

"If you were playing better, you'd have had a goal and *four* assists tonight," Walter said. Wayne grinned. Walter had turned it around, too.

Kings fans were thrilled that Wayne kept playing. In 1993, Wayne led LA to the Stanley Cup finals. It was the first time in Kings history. They lost to the Montreal Canadiens. But Wayne felt proud. He was the scoring leader in the playoffs. He'd done his best.

Chapter 11
Last Years on Ice

By the end of 1995, Wayne had played in Los Angeles for almost eight seasons. The Kings never made it to the finals again.

Now he and Janet had two more children. Ty was born in 1990, Trevor in 1992. Wayne was turning thirty-five.

He didn't have many hockey years left. And he wanted to play for a team that could win the Stanley Cup. The Kings agreed to a trade, and Wayne went to the St. Louis Blues. On July 22, 1996,

Wayne signed a two-year deal with the New York Rangers. New Yorkers welcomed Wayne with open arms.

Even better, his old friend Mark Messier was captain. Back when they were nineteen, they never dreamed they'd be playing in New York, even appearing together on talk shows.

That year, the Rangers made the playoffs.

They lost to Philadelphia in the Eastern Conference finals. It was a good effort. Wayne looked forward to doing even better next season. But things changed. Mark left to play for Vancouver.

Now many looked to Wayne for the team's success. It was a heavy burden. Wayne was in his late thirties. Many other Rangers were older, too. The team didn't make the playoffs for the next two years.

But the Rangers weren't Wayne's only team. In 1998, Wayne got the chance of a lifetime: to be part of the Winter Olympics.

For the first time, NHL players could play for their countries. Before, only amateurs could be on Olympic teams. Wayne, of course, played for Canada. That year, the Olympics were held in Nagano, Japan. Japanese Gretzky fans went wild when he stepped off the airplane. Wayne was having fun. He loved staying in the Olympic village with his teammates and other athletes.

The Canadian team had a strong start. But in the end, they didn't medal. Some say it was the coach's fault. In an overtime shoot-out, he didn't put Wayne in the lineup.

Even with these disappointments, Wayne was still a force on the ice. He was still an all-star. Still team MVP. But Wayne wanted to retire while he was on top. So 1999 would be Number Ninety-Nine's last year.

Wayne's very last game was in New York. He tried to keep to his usual routine. Family and friends had come to New York. Like so many times before, Wayne drove to the game with his dad.

At Madison Square Garden, the stands were packed. Farewell signs dotted the rows. Mark Messier was there, and so was Glen Sather, the Oilers' old coach.

For Wayne, the Canadian anthem played. One line was changed from "We stand on guard for thee," to "We're going to miss you, Wayne Gretzky." Then came "The Star-Spangled Banner." The singer switched the words "the land of the free" to "the land of Wayne Gretzky."

Before the game even began, commissioner Gary Bettman retired Wayne's number. No other hockey player would wear ninety-nine—ever! Then the commissioner spoke about the Hockey Hall of Fame. He said they'd change the rules for Wayne. He didn't have to wait years to be admitted. He was practically in right then—before he was even officially retired!

The game went into double overtime. Wayne scored his final point, number 2,857, on an assist. It was the Rangers' only goal. And the Rangers lost to the Pittsburgh Penguins.

At the end, the sellout crowd rocked the Garden. On their feet, they chanted Wayne's name.

OLYMPIC HOCKEY

THE FIRST OLYMPIC HOCKEY TOURNAMENT TOOK PLACE IN 1920 AT THE *SUMMER* OLYMPICS! CANADA WON GOLD. FOUR YEARS LATER, MEN'S HOCKEY OFFICIALLY BECAME A WINTER SPORT, AND CANADA WON AGAIN. CANADIANS WOULD DOMINATE FOR THE NEXT FOUR DECADES. THEN THE SOVIET UNION (A FORMER COUNTRY MADE UP OF RUSSIA, UKRAINE, BELARUS, AND OTHERS) JOINED THE COMPETITION. FROM 1964 TO 1988, THE SOVIETS WON SIX OUT OF SEVEN GOLD MEDALS.

IN 1980, IN THE BIGGEST UPSET IN OLYMPIC HISTORY, THE SOVIETS LOST TO THE UNITED STATES. THE AMERICANS WERE AN UNKNOWN TEAM MADE UP OF MOSTLY COLLEGE STUDENTS. CALLED "THE MIRACLE ON ICE," THE GAME HAS BEEN THE SUBJECT OF MOVIES AND BOOKS. WOMEN'S HOCKEY DIDN'T BECOME AN OLYMPIC SPORT UNTIL 1998.

Wayne hugged Jaramir Jagr, the Penguin who scored the winning goal. Then, his eyes brimming with tears, he took a final lap around the rink. His good-bye— alone, and in the spotlight—took  fifteen minutes. The fans wouldn't let him leave.

Finally, Wayne headed to the locker room. He took off his skates. Then he sat down, still in his uniform. When he took that off, he knew it would really be over.

"This is not a passing on," he told a friend later. "It's a moving on."

Chapter 12
Still the Greatest

When Wayne retired, Paulina was ten, Ty eight, and Trevor six. The family settled in California. Wayne went to his kids' games and school events. He and Janet had a normal life, just like they talked about when they met. And just like they wanted, they had a big family. Son Tristan and daughter Emma were born in 2000 and 2003.

But Wayne couldn't leave professional hockey just yet.

In February 2001, Wayne became part owner of the Phoenix Coyotes. Four years later, he was named head coach. He worked with the organization until 2009.

During that time, Wayne flew back and forth to be with his family in California. Janet and the kids visited him, too.

Those years, and all the years after he stopped playing, had many special moments. Wayne was named Hockey Player of the Century by *Sports Illustrated*.

He coached Canada's hockey team to gold in the 2002 Olympics in Salt Lake City, Utah. He lit the Olympic torch in Vancouver in 2010. He even met Queen Elizabeth II of England.

But there were sad, trying times as well. Wayne's mom, Phyllis, died in December 2005. Like Wayne, Phyllis liked to stay behind the scenes. But Wayne called her "the glue" that held the family together. Shaken up, Wayne took a leave from the Coyotes to be with her at the end.

Wayne isn't involved in pro hockey any longer. But he hasn't slowed down. He owns a Toronto restaurant, Wayne Gretzky's. It serves pierogi and other dishes like his grandmother made. He owns wineries, too. They feature bottles from the "No. 99 Collection." He has his own charity foundation to help young hockey players, and hockey camps where he plays with fans.

Wayne travels between California and Canada to be close with everyone in his family. His kids are growing up. Ty plays for a Chicago Cubs minor league baseball team. Paulina is building a career as a singer. But everyone gathers by the lakeside home in Idaho every summer.

Still, Wayne doesn't rule out returning to the NHL, as a coach or an owner. After all, he says, "I owe everything I have to hockey." And hockey owes Wayne Gretzky, too. The Oilers' equipment manager, Lyle Kulchisky, might have said it best in an ESPN documentary: "[Wayne's] always been a better person than he's been a hockey player. When you really get to know him, then you know why they call him the Great One."

TIMELINE OF WAYNE GRETZKY'S LIFE

1961	Wayne Douglas Gretzky born, January 26
1963	Puts on ice skates for first time
1968	At age seven, ends first season scoring one goal
1975	Moves to Toronto, joins Junior B team
1977	Plays in Ste. Sault Marie with Junior A team
1978	Goes pro with Indianapolis Racers
1979	Traded to Edmonton Oilers
1982	Scores fifty goals in thirty-nine games
1984	Leads Oilers to first Stanley Cup
1988	Leads Oilers to fourth Stanley Cup Marries Janet Jones Traded to Kings
1994	Becomes all-time leading goal scorer
1996	Traded to St. Louis Blues Signs with New York Rangers
1998	Plays for Canada in the Nagano Olympics
1999	Retires from playing
2001	Joins Phoenix Coyotes organization
2002	Coaches Team Canada for Olympic gold
2010	Lights Olympic torch in Vancouver

TIMELINE OF THE WORLD

John F. Kennedy is inaugurated as the thirty-fifth US president Hockey Hall of Fame opens in Toronto	1961
Zip codes introduced in the United States Beatles release first album	1963
Civil rights leader Martin Luther King Jr. is assassinated	1968
Microsoft founded by Bill Gates and Paul Allen	1975
Star Wars opens in movie theaters	1977
Susan B. Anthony dollar coin is issued Margaret Thatcher is elected prime minister of the United Kingdom	1979
USA Today first published	1982
Space shuttle *Discovery* makes its first flight	1984
Australia celebrates its bicentennial (two hundredth birthday)	1988
Channel Tunnel ("The Chunnel") opens, connecting England and France	1994
US president Bill Clinton elected to second term	1996
Bicyclist Lance Armstrong wins first of seven Tour de France championships; titles later taken away for drug use	1999
9/11: terrorists hijack four US airplanes, crashing them into the World Trade Center, the Pentagon, and a field in Pennsylvania	2001
Kelly Clarkson wins first *American Idol*	2002
The tallest building in the world, the 163-story Burj Khalifa in Dubai, United Arab Emirates, opens	2010

BIBLIOGRAPHY

* Doeden, Matt. **Wayne Gretzky**. Sports Heroes and Legends. Minneapolis, MN: Lerner Publishing Group, 2007.

Gretzky, Wayne, with John Davidson. **99: My Life in Pictures**. Toronto: Total Sports Canada, 1999.

Gretzky, Wayne, with Rick Reilly. **Gretzky: An Autobiography**. New York: HarperCollins Publishers, 1990.

* Morrison, Jessica. **Wayne Gretzky: Greatness on Ice**. St. Catharines, Ontario: Crabtree Publishing, 2011.

* Redmond, Gerald. **Wayne Gretzky: The Great One**. Toronto: ECW Press, 1993.

Sports Illustrated. **The Great One: The Complete Wayne Gretzky Collection**. Toronto: Fenn/McClelland & Stewart, 2012.

*Books for young readers

WEBSITES

www.gretzky.com

www.NHL.com

www.hhof.com (Hockey Hall of Fame)

TOP RECORDS

CAREER:
  Most points: 2,857
  Most goals: 894
  Most assists: 1,963
  Most games with three or more goals: 50

SEASON:
  Most points: 215
  Most goals: 92 (also second, with 87)
  Most assists: 163
  Most games with three or more goals: 10

PLAYOFFS:
  Most goals in career: 122
  Most assists in career: 260
  Most points in a career: 382
  Most points in a season: 47
  Most games with three or more goals: 10

  Most consecutive scoring titles: 7
  Most consecutive MVP titles: 8